D0648530

The acquisition of this volume was made possible
through a generous contribution to the Library's
GIFT OF READING program.

GIVEN IN MEMORY OF:

Jotham Pierce, Sr., Esq.

HANDWRITING ANALYSIS
MADE EASY

Quickly Discover
PERSONALITY AND BEHAVIOR TRAITS
Personally and Professionally

Jess E. Dines

Copyright ©1990 by Pantex International Ltd.

All rights reserved. No part of this book may be reproduced or transmitted in any form, or by any means, electronic, or mechanical, including photocopying, recording or by any information storage and retrieval system without prior written permission from the publisher.

First Printing — October 1990
Printed in the United States of America.

ISBN No. 0-9627666-0-7

Published by

Pantex International Ltd.
P. O. Box 17322
Irvine, CA 92713

While every effort has been made to present factual and accurate information, the author and publisher assume no responsibility or liability of any kind for anyone utilizing this information.

DEDICATION

*To Eva and Dr. Gary Dines
and those wonderful grandchildren
Jeffrey, Jennifer, Alexander and ?*

PREFACE

Unfortunately, many associate graphology (handwriting analysis) with palm reading, fortune telling , ESP, astrology and the occult. Go to any book store and try to buy a book on graphology. Most won't ever have any in stock and those that do, store them in one of the aforementioned sections.

Although it has been in existence as far back as the Egyptian Empire, its real recognition and usefullness is about 100 years old and is considered to be a science by Western countries, mostly by Europeans. Yet more and more it is being fully recognized in the U.S.A. as can be evidenced by its use in the large corporations when hiring people and those in the police, penal, legal and education professions, just to mention a few.

This book is written to "Spread The Gospel" about graphology in order for all of us to enjoy and take advantage of its usefullness. The more of us that take a decided interest in it, the more its acceptance.

Painstaking efforts were made to take the complexity out of this science (and complex it is) so that we can all understand and learn it and apply it to personal and practical use.

TABLE OF CONTENTS

INTRODUCTION

Why This Book?

There have been many books written on handwriting analysis (graphology), mostly categorically and usually consisting of hundreds of pages, laboriously explaining its intricate details. Specifically, this book is a simplified version designed for all, including the business person and professional who will find it an invaluable tool and a *must*. Such people are not likely to have the time or inclination to study and understand the full essence of graphology, especially if there is a great deal of complex reading material. Thus, this book is designed to give one a quick "thumb-nail" sketch of certain pertinent traits to look for in one's handwriting, such as drive, ambition, honesty/dishonesy, intelligence, leadership, best type of job one would be happy or suited for, how well one gets along with others, how good a manager one is, etc. Obviously, understanding solely the contents of this book will not make you a graphologist in the wildest of one's imagination, rather it serves to give you an "idea" or "feel" about someone in the fastest possible and most accurate way. To become a proficient or master graphologist takes many years of training.

In the analysis, keep in mind that anyone's particular trait is not one that necessarily occurs 100% of the time. For example, a person who is considered frugal may only be so say 70% of the time, whereas 30% of the time one may in fact be relatively generous to others. Actually such percentages may even vary continuously. So when certain traits are identified, it simply implies that they occur for the majority of the time.

Also, trait evaluation cannot be limited alone to skills and abilities but also to personality. One can be the most responsible, honest, adept person in existence, but coupled with a negative, abusive and critical personality such a person cannot coexist peacefully with others and keep "harmony" in a team-concept establishment. For example, a highly-skilled moody and depressed worker is usually counter-productive in a company because of his demoralizing effect on others.

Specifically this book is for the entrepreneur, executive, manager, supervisor, politician, and those involved in police, education, legal, medical and penal work. Also, included are those who are in purchasing, sales, engineering, personnel, credit and collections (e.g., is one a good risk?), accounting, bookkeeping, and all those involved in a leadership role such as in the military or in an academy. In actuality, this book is for *everyone* since we all want to know more about ourselves and others in personal, friendship and marital relationships.

This analysis is for those who want to know more about people with whom they are dealing, those whom they want to hire or promote, those where agreements and contracts must be signed, those who want to advance or replace others in key or responsible positions, and above all to know themselves better. It is a fact that we tend to forget and block out our bad points and amplify our good ones.

Think of the money saved in wasted training for a person who won't fit the bill. What about the attorney who wants to quickly size up his client? Is he telling the truth? Will he pay the bill? Or the doctor who wants to know if his patient is really ill or is just a hypochondriac. Such an analysis is analagous to going to a psychiatrist and giving him a chart of how you feel at the moment.

Consider, for example, when hiring or meeting someone new. First impressions are through appearance, actions and first words spoken. These can be deceptive as one can readily relate to. Couldn't a reticent, insecure person mask his personality by acting? What about a very intelligent person who is book but not street smart? Many dishonest people can look you straight in the eye and give the illusion of impeccable honesty.

What is Graphology?

Graphology is a complete, accurate examination and evaluation of behavior and personality of one's innerself, as well as others. If people really completely and thoroughly knew and understood each other (impossible!), counselling, psychiatry and psychology would be unnecessary and graphology would only divulge those obvious characteristics already known. Each of us is really three people, that is; one's self-image, the personality projected to everyone else, and a combination of all of these.

It is an inexact science (analagous to meterology) which obviously is not 100% accurate at all times. This is partly true because our behavior and personality changes daily and even sometimes instantaneously. Thus, an absolute "true" analysis would involve taking many handwriting samples over many months, and the overall results would depend upon such factors as our changing mood, environment, business/living conditions, physical/mental health, etc.

What Does Graphology Do?

It is probably the fastest way one can learn about another's behavior and personality with great accuracy. Other methods are longer, tedious, more nebulous and inaccurate. These include: written, oral and physical tests which cover personality, aptitude, intelligence and muscular coordination and even the Rorschach test.

Graphology can quickly reveal such things as your character, emotions, intellect, creativity, social adjustment, material values, physical/mental disabilities, self-awareness, reliability and physical aptitude, (sports, dancing, sex) just to mention a few.

Certainly humans are complex from the emotional point of view. Thus, in analyzing them, one should not make a sweeping statement, for example, that "one is very emotional" because first of all this is a relative statement. Secondly, one's emotions change from day to day, sometimes even from minute to minute. Emotions, of course, also depend upon other factors such as one's physical being, environment, contact with others, etc. The point is that when we characterize one as having a certain degree of emotion or of any other trait, we speak of it here as one occurring "most of the time."

Why Use Graphology?

Graphology saves you time and money since without its use, performing written and oral tests are very laborious. They are usually given well after the fact, for example, after a person is hired, accepting a new client, or signing a contract. Think of the problems and aggravation created trying to undo such acts. It is easy to jump to wrong conclusions about a stranger after one short meeting, especially if you rely mostly on your initial observations and intuitiveness. Those having undesirable traits are well-equipped and experienced to hide

10

them. They practice doing this continually and are usually very good at it.

How Does Graphology Work?

Handwriting is an instantaneous photograph of your mind. Your nervous system acts as a wire from brain to hand. Your muscles are coordinated in a more or less writing movement. It begins with a thought in your brain which is transmitted to a central nervous system and then to your hand and fingers, the latter of which are only the vehicles that put it in writing. Proof of point! During the Vietnam War, many paraplegics who lost both of their hands and arms learned to write by using a pen in their mouths. After several years of practice, this handwriting closely resembled their original one.

Just like fingerprints, no two handwritings are identical. This is true because there are endless types of strokes, sizes, formations, margins, connections, rhythms, loops, uniformity, crossings, slants, angles, pressure, space, capitals, signatures, baselines, and crossing bars which will be discussed in detail.

The following are facts you should know. One cannot tell the age through handwriting although immaturity can be seen regardless of one's chronological age. Also one cannot tell one's sex, although some masculine and feminine character-istics can be revealed. Other things that cannot be shown are one's race, religion, natural origin and even if one is left- or right-handed.

A particular trait may come out to be different in different handwritings. For example, a person who writes in a "wavy" fashion can be either nervous, energetic, diplomatic or does not know which direction he is heading in life, or any combination of these. The actual characteristics depend on other aspects of the writing like pressure, slant, size, etc.

Furthermore, a certain writing will yield certain characteristics one time and the same writing may yield other characteristics at another time since one's behavior and personality are in a constant state of flux. The approach of this book is to analyze specific parts of the writing like letters and words, and then concluding what the "over-all" signifies. It is like putting pieces of a jig-saw puzzle together.

How To Use This Book

For any particular category (such as zones, slants, pressure, and size) you will find many descriptive words associated with it. Simply read these to get a "feel" or "overall picture" of the kind of person being described. Do not dwell on only one or a few of these words.

In fact, some of these may even appear to be contradictory or unrelated. For example, one who writes small may be meticulous, restrained, modest, thrifty, reticent or reluctant just to mention a few of the traits. It is possible but unlikely that one would possess all of these. Yet if the same person also writes to the left possessing such traits as: being introverted, non-communicative, insensitive, inhibited, defiant, insecure, independent, we begin to see a picture of the narrowing down and minimizing the others as to what traits this person really has by "combining" those similar traits. Further combining still other traits will narrow it down even further, zeroing in to final conclusions as to this person's character and personality.

Some traits can simultaneously exist for different aspects of handwriting (there's an overlap). For example, writing to the left as well as the suppression of the lower zone could have the same traits of fear, defiance, introversion and repression. Either one of these aspects usually has the same traits. Having both means "more so"; *one alone* means there is only a "tendency," but not necessarily.

The Handwriting Sample

The more you can get of a handwriting sample, the better. For a quick but not necessarily a very accurate picture, even a small sample on scrap paper (avoid napkins if possible) might do. A pen or pencil will suffice, although the former is preferable. Two or more pages of 8 x 11 unlined paper is ideal, although more often than not you will have to settle for less. If the paper is lined, the writing should be against the lines. If possible, do not tell one that the handwriting is being analyzed since it could be changed intentionally. Avoid analyzing handwriting on envelopes. A signature must always follow the handwriting sample (but never a signature alone), since this is not nearly enough for a complete fair analysis.

Tell one to write whatever comes into one's mind and in this way you could check one's creativity and intelligence among other things. Such sentences as "Yipee! I dig the free drinks," is very revealing through the use of pertinent letters as will be shown. "How," not "what" one writes, is what should be analyzed.

Some people insist on printing instead of writing. Simply indicate that if one can sign one's name (we all can sign checks, hopefully), then one can write instead of print. Look for slant, size, speed, pressure, capital and small letters, line of writing, beginning and ending strokes, style, margins and signature.

13

Also, since some people write differently at different times, then their analysis also differs at these times.

If you know the person being analyzed, try not to pre-judge his traits. You could be wrong. Several analyses may be necessary since one changes his writing depending upon how he feels physically and mentally at the moment.

Chapter 1

SLANT

Slant signifies one's emotions. It determines the degree of emotional expression and social behavior. The slant one uses has absolutely nothing to do with whether a writer is right-handed or left-handed.

A. *Towards Right:*

(relatively self-emotional) extroverted, warm personality, communicative, affectionate, amicable, compassionate, gregarious, courageous, expressive, sensitive, sympathetic, future-and-goal oriented, lives life with "zest," needs to be with others, always wants "something going on," cries and laughs more readily, easily vents feelings.

NOTE: Writing only slightly to right can be considered to be an "ideal" slant from the emotional point of view.

I have do
and I thoug
interesting!

B. *Towards Left:*

(back-handed writers): cautious, suspicious, withdrawn, very little or non-existent self-emotion, introverted, cold personality, non-communicative, unaffectionate, unfriendly, non-compassionate, unexpressive, insensitive, unsympathetic, "lives in past," lives life in a withdrawn way, a "loner," not interested in being with others, hardly ever vents feelings, rarely laughs or cries, shy, inhibited, difficult to figure out, defiant, has anxiety, independent, "hides from life," fearful, depressed.

NOTE: Such writers hardly ever openly show these adverse traits for fear they will be found out and have learned well on how to hide these. Of course, they will never admit to such traits.

C. Vertical Slant:

(characteristics are the median between the right and left slants.) Ambivert, restrained, emotions in check, independent, self-reliant, secure, self-controlled, "head rules heart."

NOTE: Such writing is good for managers, drill sergeants and police personnel.

D. Extreme Right:

(same as for the right except to the extreme): bombastic, emotional reactions, extremely insecure, (very) passionate, jealous, hateful, possessive, suspicious, insecure, restless, unsettled, impulsive, capable of hysteria, an "emotional" bonfire.

16

NOTE: Fortunately, such writing is rare and such a writer could very well be emotionally ill.

E. Extreme Left:

(same as for the left except to the extreme): insecure, fear of life itself, completely withdrawn emotionally, out of touch with reality, lives almost entirely in past.

NOTE: Fortunately, such writing is rare and such a writer could very well be emotionally ill.

F. Varying Or Eratic Slant:

Doesn't know in which "direction" in life to go, unsettled, erratic emotional behavior, inconsistent moods and thoughts, goes from repression to expression, undisciplined, nervous, excitable, fickle, lacks proper judgement, inferiority complex.

Notes

Chapter 2
SIZE OF SCRIPT

Script size paints a picture of how relatively small or large our thoughts and life experiences are.

A. *Small Size:*

Thinks small, sees life through a microscope, meticulous, great in "detail" work, restrained, reticent, modest, perfectionist, resourceful, thrifty, reluctant, mentally academic, doesn't seek limelight, not very communicative, good organizer, good executive ability.

B. *Large Size:*

Bold, aggressive, thinks "big," confident, strongly motivated and directs others, approaches life in an extroverted and exaggerated manner, wants and needs attention, needs recognition, wants admiration, needs people, enthusiastic, optimistic, likes to boast, lacks concentration and discipline.

NOTE: Bold writing means bold behavior in thought and action.

19

C. *Middle Size:*

(the "in-between" of small and large sizes) "middle of the road" attitude, secure, conservative, lawful, traditional, conformist, conventional, adaptable, practical, realistic.

I am very in
more about a
I welcome to

D. *Variable Size:*

Indecisive, moody, naive, immature, inconsistent, self-centered, "off balance" emotionally.

730 Am. They ha
to be in to work
I'll leave key on
tank — wk

Chapter 3

SPACING
Between Words, Lines and Letters

A. Spacing Between Words:
   Represents the physical and mental contact (or distance) between one's self and others (society).

• **Normal** – Physical and mental contact is acceptable to all others

• **Very Narrow Spacing** – needs contact and closeness with others, self-centered, selfish, "crowds" others for attention.

It was a very emotional

• **Very Wide Spacing** – need for inner privacy and "space," tendency for isolation, difficulty in communicating with others, wants to maintain distance from social contact.

is lovely

B. Spacing Between Lines:

   The amount is directly proportional to orderliness, thought clarity, and interaction one wishes to have with the environment and society.

21

- **Normal** – Personal harmony, flexibility and proper balance.

people to realize
different people
dig the fig tree

- **Lines Far Apart From Each Other** – isolates oneself from the environment and society both psychologically and/or socially, suspicious, fear of contact and closeness, hostile, extravagant. *dig the fig tree*

is a beautiful

- **Lines Close To Each Other** –Wants close interaction with the environment and society. When lines are extremely close to one another, there is fear of isolation and distance. Can also mean a lack of clarity of thoughts and feeling, poor concentration, constant need of expressing oneself in words and actions, forceful, creative.

- **Lines Tangled (One Line Runs Into The Other)** – Confused about thoughts and feelings, poor concentration although lively, forceful and creative. Such a person suffers from lack of clarity.

went to the
at the ?
found it to ?

C. Spacing Between Letters:

● **Normal** – "balanced" personality, ability to make friends and be close to others, flexible.

That is quite a story! I

● **Very Crowded** – suspicious, cautious, introverted, good concentration.

will be interested

● **Broad** – broad-minded, uninhibited, extroverted, outgoing, difficulty in concentration.

● **Narrow and Crowded** – narrow-minded, inhibited, introverted, self-conscious, tense, good concentration, frugal.

Notes

Chapter 4
ZONES

There are three zones – upper, middle and lower. The relative domination of a particular zone determines the accentuation of the traits found in this zone. Note that zones have many traits in common with slant.

A. Upper Zone:
Determines imagination, spiritualism, intensity, intellect, conscience, ambition, creativity, fantasy.

B. Lower Zone:
Determines physical and sexual drives and needs, desire for money.

C. Middle Zone:
Sphere of immediate concerns and actuality regarding social and work life (job, living quarters, meals, possessions, etc.)

D. Inflated Upper Zone:
The aforementioned upper zone traits are accentuated, that is, very great imagination, spiritualism, intellect and thought.

E. Compressed Lower Zone:
Lack and need for physical and sexual desires.

what you See!

Inflated Upper Zone/Compressed Lower Zone

F. Compressed Upper Zone:
Little interest in mental, spiritual or philosophical thought, lack of creativity, imagination or new thoughts, non-intellectual, lacks goals, lacks self-image.

G. Inflated Lower Zone:
Spends and uses much time to satisfy need for physical and sexual desires, need for money, willful.

Yyppee I dig the free drinks

Compressed Upper Zone/Inflated Lower Zone

H. Inflated Middle Zone:
Overly concerned with one's daily needs, makes "mountains out of a mole hill," immature, conceited, gets bored easily, feels confined.

up and shabby; but

26

I. Compressed Middle Zone:

Everyday social and worklife concerns relatively unimportant.

Show me a

the list one more

NOTE: An equal balance of all three zones indicates a balance of one's inner equilibrium and maturity and basic stability. It also indicates a healthy ego, how well one's ability is to get along with others, accomplishing set goals and is generally well-adjusted to life.

Notes

Chapter 5
PRESSURE

Pressure gives a picture of one's energy and intensity of thought—such as the magnitude of alertness, drive, craving, persistence, imagination, perception, will-power, perseverance, warmth, stubborness, sensitivity, self-control, sense of humor, discipline, determination, sensuality, just to mention some.

A. Heavy Pressure:
Indicates that energy and intensity of thought is greatly accentuated. Such writers are very aggressive, possessive, go-getters, success-oriented, have tempers, can be verbally abusive, have a big ego, are altruistic towards their family, may even be violent, tend to have high blood pressure.

ve to fin

B. Light Pressure:
Fragile, delicate feelings, sensitive personality, weak will-power, more tolerant.

C. Medium Pressure:
It is the "mean" or balance between heavy and light pressure. Has moderate energy and intensity of thought, is cooperative, blends well socially, is relatively calm and can be classified as a "middle-of-the-roader."

been reading

D. Varying Heavy and Light Pressure:

Can be emotionally disturbed, moody, frustrated, tormented and unduly aggressive.

Chapter 6
GENERAL TYPES

Certain "styles" of writing reveal specific personality types.

A. Garland *lurken luil*

Identified at the bottom part of the script where letters are concave-like and form a cup or arc.

Good – affable, even-tempered, charming, gracious, receptive, responsive, "open," flexible, diplomatic, avoids conflict, socially adaptable, pleasure-loving, likeable, kind, sympathetic, outgoing.

Bad – passive, indifferent, dislikes life "changes," wants acceptance by others, can be lazy, gullible or insecure, lacks restraint.

Also – noncompetitive, conventional.

B. Arcade *Sunday cole*

Identified at the top part of the script by convex-like letters.

Good – creative, gentle, obedient, nonaggressive, gets along mostly well with others, can be authoritative but not domineering, good memory, protective.

Bad – procrastinates, usually eccentric, privately a rebel, gullible, slow to memorize, can be immature, only accepts gradual changes, can be dominated, tries to "shut" out real world, concealing.

Also – traditionalist, relies on intuitiveness rather than objectivity, conformist.

Such writing is often found in the "arts," including artists, sculptors, theatrical people.

C. *Angular*

Good – tends to substitute intellect for emotions, analytical, logical, firm, steadfast, goal-oriented, energetic, shrewd, very determined, great drive, ambitious, determined to succeed, competitive.

Bad – forceful, rigid, stubborn, argumentative, critical, self-centered, indifferent, vindictive, has difficulty giving love, praise and affection.

Also – aggressive, willful, assertive, disciplinary.

Such writing is often identified with engineers and scientists; also such writers make excellent "strategists" in any walk of life.

D. *Threaded*

This is the most difficult to analyze since such formations can also be attributed to haste or impatience.

Good – versatile, innovative, independent, broad-minded, intuitive, seek appreciation rather than rewards, highly intelligent or "genius" type, perceptive, adaptable.

Bad – insecure, impatient, has nervous tension, fearful, undisciplined, unpredictable, cannot be "pinned" down, impatient, indecisive, can be dishonest.

Also – very sensitive and curious. Such writers often have a love for the "arts" and make good teachers and social workers.

Notes

Chapter 7

INDIVIDUAL LETTERS

The first and natural tendency for one learning graphology is to come to conclusions by noting the way a certain letter is written. Sometimes this is true (especially with the letters "I" and "T"), but realistically it should only help in the final analysis where all facets of the writing should be considered before forming the final conclusions. Since it would be too voluminous to give every type of letter variation analysis, only the important ones will be given here. Whereas, conventional forms indicate conventional behavior, ornamental and decorative signs show creativeness in the arts and weird types are indicative of weird thought and behavior. Complicated letters means getting involved and solving problems.

A. *Capitals*

Capital letters represent the "public" side of the writer, that is, the way he wants others to see him, like signatures. The greater the size of capitals of the script, the greater the confidence, pride and vanity; the reverse is true for small capitals. Ornamental capitals show ostentation and self-consciousness. Capitals which show originality and grace are indicative of artistry and creativeness. Printed capitals are indicative of one being constructive.

B. The Capital Letter "I"

The capital 'I' is literally a picture of what the writer secretly thinks of himself. It reveals one's ego, self-image and self-worth.

When Inflated – great pride, inflated ego, tries to be impressive and creative, imaginative, vain.

When Deflated – deflated ego, inferiority complex.

Left Tilting – has fear and mistrust, standoffish, over-modest, insecure, defensive, rebellious, guilt feelings, lack of self-confidence, cautious, suspicious.

Right Tilting – need for attention, praise, approval and affection, dependent upon people.

Vertical (No Tilt) – independent, unemotional, self-sufficient, demands privacy.

Printed "I" – constructive, good taste, independent, modest, versatile.

Large Straight Vertical Line "I" (best kind) – confident, independent, self-sufficient, self-satisfying, no need nor is influenced by anyone (especially parents), emotionally self-supporting, practical, clear, concise, strong and firm ego.

Inflated Underloops – gregarious, outgoing, vain, imaginative, loves attention, self-conscious.

36

Flourishes (Unneeded Extra Lines, Loops, etc.) –tries to prove to the world of one's confidence and ego, overestimates oneself, flamboyant, time waster, unwarrantedly considers oneself to be creative.

Different "I's" – versatile.

C. The Small Letter "i" (also "j")

It is a measure of both concentration and imagination. The higher the dot from the body, the greater the imagination. The closer the dot, the greater the attention to detail, concentration, memory and enthusiasm.

Dot Placed High Above Stem – good imagination, spiritual.

Circled Dots – needs attention, loyal, interested in the arts, faddish.

Wavy Dots – sense of humor, fun-loving.

Dots Placed Before The Stem – timid, cautious, procrastinates, afraid to start anything new.

Dashed Dot – enthusiastic, has drive, could be cruel and irritable.

Dot At Right Of Stem – impulsive, impatient, quick.

Absence of Dot – absent-minded, poor memory, careless.

Tall and Sharp-Pointed Stem – sharp, quick, penetrating mind.

Loopy Stems – lazy, slow, careful.

Tent-Shaped – temper, brutal, critical.

Arrow-Shaped – cruel, sarcastic, irritable, domineering.

D. The Letter "t"

"t" tells all and is the most revealing letter, more specifically the bar crossing the stem. There are scores of different ways to cross a "t" which changes even minute-by-minute as one's emotions, personality and health changes. A mixture of t-bars indicates the writer has conflicting views and goals and is either versatile or unpredictable.

Bar Positions

Average Balanced Crossing – balanced, self-controlled, calm, firm.

Crosses Left Of Stem – procrastinates, indecisive, lives in the past.

Crosses Right Of Stem – impulsive, enthusiastic, energetic, rebellious.

Down-Slanted – argumentative, fearful, despondent, destructive, cruel.

Up-Slanted – optimistic, enthusiastic, ambitious.

Above Stem – spiritual, imaginative, dreamer, has fantasies.

Low On the Stem – inferiority complex, low goals.

Light Pressure – indecisive, sensitive, resigned, timid, "weak" person.

Heavy Pressure – domineering, great energy, insensitive, aggressive, powerful.

Short Crossing – lacks drive and willpower.

Long Crossing – energetic, bold, ambitious, persistent, confident, bossy, enthusiastic.

No Crossing – absent-minded, hasty, careless, rebellious.

Sharp-Ending ("Dagger") – sarcastic, critical, verbally "sticks" to hurt others.

Club-Like Ending – brutal, blunt, domineering, verbally "hits" (like a club) to hurt others.

Bowed-Bar – protective, inhibited, self-controlled, self-disciplined.

39

Inverted Bowed-Bar – open, gullible, shallow, fickle, unstable, guilt-complex.

Wavy Bar – sense of humor, good-natured, gracious, intuitive.

Star-Like T – stubborn, sensitive.

"Tented" – defensive, cautious.

Return-Stroke To Left – wants to live in past, not confident, introverted, insecure.

Blunt Ending – unyielding.

Down-Turned Hook – bitter, seeks revenge.

Up-Turned Hook – stubborn, tenacious.

Knotted – tenacious, persistent, logical.

Also

"Old-Fashioned" T – afraid to start something new.

Looped Stem – self-sensitive.

E. *Going Through The Rest Of The Alphabet (Small Letters)*

1. "a" and "o" (and lower part of "d")

Double-Looped – insincere, lies sometimes, sly, crafty, may be dishonest (could possibly apply to single loop).

Open At Top – gullible, generous, open-minded, talkative, outgoing, hard to keep a secret, sincere, (if tightly closed) cautious, reticent.

Open At Bottom – probably dishonest (many embezzlers write this way).

Having A Lead-In Stroke – worrier.

2. "b"

Bottom Portion Is Open – gullible, trusting

Bottom Portion Is Tightly Closed – cautious, suspicious, business-sense, secretive.

Very Loopy Top Stroke – very emotional.

3. "c"

"Crowns" or Loops – vain, pretentious, some rigidity, could be artistic.

41

4. "d"

Loopy Stem – self-sensitive, (the wider the loop, the greater the sensitivity).

Tall-Unlooped Stem – independent, dignity, pride, has "mental" penetration.

Short-Unlooped Stem – modest, humble, cautious, reduced mental interest (if too short, very low ego).

Very Tall And Wide Loop – super-sensitive, vain, arrogant, conceited.

Split Stem – cautious, reticent, lazy, stubborn.

"Spoon" Stem – independent, creative, cultural, altruistic, pleasure-loving, flirtatious.

5. "e"

Closed Loop – cautious, suspicious, secretive, skeptical (when filled in - sensuous).

Broad Loop – talkative, broadminded, blunt.

Greek "E" – cultured, likes refined tastes.

6. "f" - related to organization and planning

f   **Balanced Upper And Lower Parts** – organized, balanced, poised, planner.

f   **No Upper Loop** – opinionated, practical, abrupt.

f   **Large Lower Loop** – physical, sexual, sports-oriented.

f   **Angular** – opinionated, stubborn.

f   **Fluid Form** – altruistic, pleasure-loving, quick mind.

f   **Knotted** – tenacious, persistent, logical.

7. "g," "q," "y," and "z" - Stems

g - y   **Long-Stem Length** – physical, sexual, sports-oriented.

g - y   **Over-Fullness Of Stem (Phallic Symbol)** – gregarious, strong sex drive, loves money.

g y   **No Or Very Narrow Long Loop** – has no-nonsense approach, practical, aggressive.

g y   **Triangular Stems** – opinionated, critical, tenacious, has drive, aggressive, compulsive.

Minimal Or Incompletion Of Bottom Loop – may be sexually frustrated, or could have sexual aberrations

"g" Written Like Number "9" – mathematical ability, superior judgment, could have sexual aberrations

"g" Written Like Number "8" – intellectual, altruistic, adaptable, quick thinking, understanding, good with numbers.

8. "h," "k," and "l" - Loops

Short Loops – reduced mental reach, immature, lazy, indifferent, materialistic.

Tall Narrow Loops – spiritual, high mental reach, curiosity, reserve, strong opinions.

Tall And Wide – seeks greater social interests.

Pointed Loop – penetrating mind, spiritual.

Single Line (No Loop) – practical, blunt, no-nonsense approach, intelligent, practical.

9. "m" and "n"

Rounded – slow, cautious, lazy, immature.

_ＷＷ_ _ＷＷ_　**Sharp Points** – high mental reach and quickness, "sharp" mind.

_ＭＬ_　**Initial Stroke Large And Flourishing** – diplomatic, executive ability.

_ＭＬ_　**Final Stroke Higher Than Any Other** – eccentric, stubborn, need for authority.

_ＭＮ_　**Graceful First Stroke** – good-natured, desire to be agreeable.

10. "r"

_ＪＬ_　**Flat-Topped** – conformity, planning ability.

_ＡＬ_　**Double-Peaked** – perceptive, clever, manual dexterity.

_ＪＬ_　**Initial Stroke "Looped"** – proud, stubborn.

_Ｒ_ _Ｒ_　**Parochial 'r'** – artistic and musical ability.

10. "s"

_Ｓ_　**Printed "s"** – artistic, cultured.

_Ａ＋Ｓ_　**Two Types** – versatility.

F. Loops

The height of a loop shows one's mental interests and spiritualism whereas the width refers to one's social and

45

gregarious nature. Most script contains a certain amount of loops in moderation indicating emotional stability and well-being. When the loops of the script are exaggerated and very loopy, the writer is generally much more emotional and has greater experience in feelings. Such persons tend to be more extroverted, compassionate, social, sympathetic, intuitive and impulsive. When the loops are extremely excessive, it is a sign of an excessive emotional need and one's feelings are bottled up. Scanty or narrow loops means repressed emotional feelings.

Tall and wide loops show mental interests and spiritualness. (A wide loop in "d" shows self-sensitivity as previously shown.)

Tall and narrow loops still show mental interests and spiritualness, but writer is more critical.

G. *Extra Strokes*

The size of the attached lead-in stroke (for a, c, d, g, m, n, and q) is directly proportional to the amount one has of worry, fear or concern about being accepted. The absence of lead-in strokes is indicative of one who is free of worry and fear and is organized, creative, intelligent, fast-thinking, mature and decisive.

An absence of ending strokes indicates one who is not a time-waster, frugal, direct, independent, self-sufficient and can concentrate. Very short endings show one to be shy, reticent, whereas very long endings show gregariousness, openness and generosity. Ending strokes which are strong indicate strong drive.

The writer whose script is ornamental, flourished and decorative wants attention, to be noticed, approved by others and is apt to be extravagant and have show-manship.

H. Knots, Hooks, and Claws

Knotted letters (see letters "t" and "f") indicate one who is tenacious, persistent and logical. Those consistently write with upturned claws and hooks like to hook or grab onto material things and money, can be greedy and are intolerant to argument or opposition and can be vindictive in eliminating it. The same applies to downturned hooks with the addition of being forceful and bitter.

Knots

Hooks

Claws

Notes

Chapter 8
SIGNATURES

The writing of our signature perceives the way we want the world (others) to see us but it is not necessarily the way we are. When the signature is the same as the script (same size, clarity, slant, etc.) then the person has no pretense and "what you see is what you get." Otherwise the signature is the way he wants us to see him, but in actuality that person is different.

Signature Smaller Than Script –

Introverted, shy, submissive, humble, mild, oversenstive, calm, insecure, unpretentious.

Signature Larger Than Script –

Extroverted, proud, healthy ego, confident, ambitious, secure, forward, wants recognition.

Signature Very Much Larger Than Script –

Writer acts overly important, very proud, ostentatious, overreacts.

Signature Slants Left—Script Slants Right –

Writer acts and wants others to see him as reserved and restrained and introverted whereas in actuality writer is outgoing, extroverted and likeable.

Signature Slants Right—Script Slants Left Or Is Vertical –

Writer acts and wants others to perceive him as extroverted, outgoing, but in actuality he is just the opposite and is actually a private person.

Signature Vertical—Script Vertical Or Slight Left Slant –

Writer is very controlled to the world as well as to himself, a "cool cat" for all to see.

Underscoring –

Writer says to the world, "Look how great I am," has ego, pride and self-confidence.

Charles Dickens   Benjamin Franklin

When Heavy: aggressive and clannish

When Curved and Smooth: charm and graciousness

When Angular: forcefulness, temper, strong personality

Illegible Signature (With Legible Writing) –

Writer communicates well but doesn't want you to know him unless he desires it. Could also be secretive, insecure, self-hatred, impatient, hostile, inconsiderate, egotistical, eccentric.

William Howard Taft

Illegible Signature (With Illegible Writing) –

Writer doesn't care if you read what he writes, could be devious or dishonest, egocentric, impatient. Writing hand cannot keep up with extremely fast mind.

Encircled Signature –

Desire to hide or shelter oneself from society, excessive secretiveness, self-interest.

Joseph Conrad

Crossed-Out Signature –

Hostility towards oneself, self-destructive.

Francisco Franco

ALSO – Large capitals indicate confidence and pride, wanting recognition. Creative signature indicates creative person (usually found in the "arts").

Signatures of Famous People

Richard Nixon
signature, from top
1968, 1969, early 1974,
late 1974.

Diahann Carroll

James Cagney

Joseph McCarthy

Henry Fonda

Franklin D. Roosevelt

52

Steve McQueen

Katherine Hepburn

Albert Einstein

Walt Disney

Marilyn Monroe

Thomas A. Edison

Ludwig Van Beethoven

Fidel Castro

Walter Cronkite

George Washington

Henry Ford, II

Abraham Lincoln

Notes

Chapter 9
HONESTY AND DISHONESTY

Honest

Such writers are categorized as legitimate, sincere, law-abiding, truthful, fair, upright, dedicated, faithful, trustworthy, loyal, courageous, have integrity, are straighforward and are free from fraud, deception, and subterfuge.

The script is clear, consistent, simple and legible, has a uniform style, a constant firm pressure, even baseline, absence of ornamental writing with extra strokes and has a consistent slant, size, spacing and pressure. In addition, the letters are well formed, the i-dot and t-bar are firm and exact, and there is no over- or under-inflated capital I. Also, the three zones are evenly balanced.

Dishonest

Such writers are unprincipled, devious, disloyal, deceptive, unfaithful; they cheat, steal, forge, lie, embezzle, conceal, spy, betray, exaggerate, lack integrity and are untrustworthy.

NOTE: Of course, no one is perfect. Each of us has a certain degree of dishonesty, insincerity, and a little larceny no matter how apparently honest we are. Also, a person may turn dishonest as a result of fear which in turn is due to anxiety, pressure or stress, or when exposed and tempted by easily obtainable money or material things. Most of us tell little white lies and at times stretch the truth to be tactful or diplomatic. The question is how much and how often. If the writer has relatively few of the following indications, one should be extremely careful in judging him adversely at all. The greater the number of the following signs, the more the chances are we are dealing with a dishonest person. A very good point to remember is that a dishonest writer sometimes "forces" himself to write differently than his mind really wants him to, especially if he knows his script gives him away. Thus, he may intentionally write too slow or too neat.

Script

Usually the script is inconsistent, varying in slant, size, spacing, pressure; baseline is erratic and illegible which can also be due to hurried writing; ornamental, complex (or even too simplistic), backhanded writing. A combination of arcade, threaded and angular writing makes one a logical suspect. More specifically, look for the following signs:

WORDS — Numerous inconsistencies and pauses between words and syllables. Claws and hooks at the beginning of words are evident.

LETTERS (AND NUMBERS) — When oval letters 'a' and 'o' (and upper portions of 'p' and 'q') are looped on the left side, there is a trace of self deception, and when looped on the right side it indicates exaggeration or flattery.

When looped on both sides and slightly open on the top, the writer tends to be insincere and not to be believed. When these letters are stenciled, dishonesty exists, which is the way many embezzlers write.

Regarding all letters and numbers, dishonesty can be shown by inconsistencies and pauses, omission of parts, broken up, slurring, tangled, retracing several times, very narrow, cramping of upper zone letters (l, b, f, h, k, I) which are normally looped, cross-stroking, beginning letter of word oversized or undersized, first letter written clearly while others are not or omitted entirely or vice-versa, some letters replaced with ones that should not be there, touching up or corrected letters, letters appearing to look like others, abrupt stops, heavy brutal downward strokes, omission or replacing of dots, dashes or letters themselves, cramped, very weak or absent T-bars, threads instead of letters, capital letters misplaced or interchanged with small letters (usually the beginning of words).

LOOPS — ink-filled, double-or-triple overinflated, excessively backward, upside down, tangled, complicated, blotchy.

STROKES — prolonged, left-tendency finals, unusual lead-in (much of those that start from below baseline) or those which begin at left and end up at right.

PRESSURE — extremely light or dark, varied, muddy, or slurry.

BASELINE – highly erratic, wavy, too rigid, sinuous, constantly variable.

NEATNESS AND CLARITY — blotchy and smeary.

SIGNATURE — script and signature completly different.

Showing Honesty

I acquired your magazine & it. says

Showing Dishonesty

Mname today. I mess my cat and dir. be good

58

Chapter 10
INTELLIGENCE

In writing, no simple curlicue or squiggle can capture one's true intelligence. An intelligent person is one who has most, if not all, of the following traits and can communicate his thoughts simply and directly; is organized, objective, intuitive, logical, pragmatic, mentally flexible, has a good memory and reasoning power, and can concentrate.

The more of these traits one has, the more intelligent. To have all makes for a potential genius.

1. Simplified Writing

No extra beginning or ending strokes. The more legible the script the better. Writers who create "short-cut" strokes show their ingenuity and creativeness in handling problems. The best example is a large straight vertical line "I." Other examples are an encircled letter, or a letter may look like a number (e.g., a "g" written as "8").

2. Organization

Shown by a balance between upper and lower loops, especially the small letter "f."

3. Objectivity

Not letting outside influences, such as emotion, prejudice or personal feeling, help make decisions. Look for some small open ovals (in a's and o's) and narrow spacing between words, letters or margins. Also, vertical writing and simple strokes.

4. *Intuitiveness*

Such a writer uses his subconscious to take mental shortcuts when forming conclusions. Can be identified by disconnected words usually after capital letters and after "i's" and "t's."

5. *Logic And Reason*

A consistent cause and effect problem solver. Just like his thoughts and in most cases the letters in the words are connected together. Also, the script is strong and even.

6. *Memory*

Can be defined as the storage and then the remembrance of one's knowledge and experiences, especially the emotional ones. A script with a good memory is one whose i-dots are precisely close and over the stem, carefully executed punctuation marks, and medium-to-heavy even pressure.

7. *Concentration*

A writer with good concentration writes like a writer with a good memory; in addition, his script is very small and legible.

8. *"Sharpness" Of Mind*

An extremely quick and articulate thinker makes him "sharp" (e.g., a good poker player or a con-man). Look for sharply-pointed letters especially m's and n's.

9. *Flexibility*

Adapting one's personality to different situations as well as to others. Such writers have a garland writing slanting to the right. You might say they "roll with the punches."

Chapter 11
LEADERSHIP

The following are leadership traits. The greater the number one has, the more the leadership potential.

1. *Determination*

This can be seen by the "down-strokes" of letters in the lower zone (especialy the letter "y," a long t-crossing). The stronger, longer, simpler and non-looped the down stroke, the greater the physical energy needed to complete a job or goal. Also, the more practical, time-saver and follow-through-to-the-end the person is.

2. *Confidence*

The more confident one is the more the self-esteem, the more secure, the less the adverse traits, such as jealousy, fear, possessiveness and suspiciousness.

The letter "I" best shows this (Chapter 7). One who is confident writes with a medium-to-large script, strong and firm pressure and with simple lettering. Capital letters are big and bold. A rapid writer as well as one who underscores signatures further exemplifies this.

3. *Communication*

One who has a goal as well as excellent command of the language. Preferably, he would possess a garland writing with some of the a's and o's only slightly open at the top. Narrow and closed a's and o's signify lack of communication.

4. Sense Of Humor

Humor paves a way of communicating situations in an easy and pleasant way. Such people write with wavy beginning strokes, especially in capital M's and N's and the dots in i's which are shaped like tents.

5. Self-Starter

Works well alone without prodding or supervision. Such a writer writes well with no beginning strokes.

Chapter 12
OTHER CHARACTERISTICS

A. *Organization*

Organization is a key element for the business and professional person for he must have the proper ability to arrange plans and causes in an orderly fashion. Good organization is associated with self-control, responsibility, planning, thought and behavior, decisiveness, stability, control over emotions and impulses.

Organized Writer

Writes with a uniform and constant regularity, evenness of spacing between letters within words as well as spacing between words, including a firm baseline and consistent and uniform size of letters and words. Bold open forms indicate a bold confident behavior.

Disorganized Writer

Writes in an opposite manner than one that is organized. Such a writer implies instability, indecisiveness and lack of self-control and direction. Such a writer writes in a tangled way indicating tangled thoughts, letters are tightly jammed indicating a narrow cautious mind and attitude (especially with a left-slant). Exaggerated writing indicates exaggerated thoughts and feelings. Closed letters (a, o, p, q) indicate secrecy and a closed mental attitude. A distorted jerky script of varying pressures, blotching, scratchouts are all negatives.

B. Printed Script

Printed script has upper and lower zones while block printing has only one zone. Although analysis is possible for these, it is beyond the scope of this book.

Most people print to obtain better clarity, legibility and precision and after a long period of time, they are more familiar with it, think faster and therefore are more comfortable using it. Such people operate more like a "mental" machine being analytical, objective and quick. They feel that goals can be accomplished with very little emotional involvement or perhaps they don't want to show their emotions. In some cases, writers print in order not to reveal their real writing for fear of "discovery," such as being introverted or dishonest. Those who mix printing with written script show versatility. They print for simple reading and switch to cursive writing to express their emotions. On the other hand, they could be confused about their social roles, feelings of expression and thought, and might be socially unstable.

C. Speed Of Writing

The speed of writing in which one writes is directly proportional to one's intelligence and intellectual ability, even genius, for such writers the hand cannot keep up with the rapid thoughts being generated. Slower writers are usually conventional and sometimes even lazy or clumsy and can be suspected of dishonesty, self-consciousness and even stupidity. For those who write so rapidly that the script can hardly be read are either dishonest or really don't care who reads it anyway.

D. *Margins*

Generally even margins on all sides indicates a balanced and organized person aware of social boundaries who has normal poise control and an aesthetic sense.

Wide Margins

When left and right margins are both wide, the person probably is extravagant, generous, needs "space." When the margin is wide only at the left, the person wants to avoid the past and has courage in facing life. When the wide margin is at right, the person wants to avoid the future, and is reserved, self-conscious and thrifty. A wide lower margin indicates one who is idealistic, reserved, aloof and one who probably loses interest easily. A wide upper margin is one who is modest and likes formality.

Narrow Margins

When both left and right margins are narrow, a person is frugal, reserved and is inconsiderate. A narrow upper margin indicates a person is direct, indifferent and prefers informality. A narrow lower margin means a person is sentimental, wants to communicate and could be materialistic.

No Margins Anywhere

Indicates a person who is insecure, frugal, talkative, and strongly influenced by others, and could fear death.

Uneven Margins (At Right)

Impulsive moods, unreliable reactions.

Uneven Margins (At Left)

Rebellious, defiant, unbalanced.

E. *Connects And Disconnects*

Connected Writing (Very Few Disconnects In Letters)

GOOD — Objective, analytical, logical, rational, calculating, strategic, persistent, goal-oriented, organized, realistic, determined, practical, has powers of concentration, has good memory.

BAD — Restless, seeks constant change, lacks concentration, bores easily, inconsiderate, tactless, compulsive, hides feelings. Such writers make good students.

Disconnected Writing

GOOD — Intuitive, sensitive, perceptive, has good memory for impressions, observant, great imagination, independent judgment, inventive, inspirational, good timing.

BAD — Egocentric, aloof, moody, inconsistent, shy, restless, selfish, insecure, cautions, suspicious, possessive, fearful, unadaptable, lonely, illogical, impractical, unreasonable, disorganized.

ALSO — Thinks in "overall" way rather than systematically.

Connections Between Words

Great powers of concentration, secretive, logical, thinks things through from one end to the other.

F. Line Slants (Shows Mood)

Straight: Steadfast, self-controlled, on even keel.

Slant Upward: Positive attitude, ambitious, lively, optimistic, restless.

Slant Downward: Negative attitude, depressed, despondent, melancholy gloomy.

Organized Writing

moved and there are
I'd rather deal

Disorganized Writing

Dick is great
Jack is fine
aren

Connected Writing

but didn't know
couldn't look it up.

Disconnected Writing

I would appreciate
product information on

Notes

Chapter 13

NOW YOU CAN ANALYZE!

It is simple as A, B, C, using the procedure outlined below.

A. For each listed "CATEGORY," simply circle those items listed in the category.

B. Refer to the text and write down all of the traits which are the most dominant in the script indicated for that part of the category.

C. You now have an "overall" picture of the handwriting being analyzed.

In many cases, several items will apply for one category. For example, in the category "SIZE OF SCRIPT" the writing can be small, large, medium or variable. Say, for instance, the script is *both* large and variable. This means that the person being analyzed can have such traits as (for LARGE SIZE) boldness, confidence, extroversion, etc., and such traits as (for VARIABLE SIZE) being indecisive, moody, naive, etc.

A continued and complete analysis of all of the other categories will narrow down the final analysis traits even further. That is, after all of the other categories are taken into consideration, a process of elimination should be used. For example, a particular trait that dominates, is one that is repeated many times (or those which are closely related) whereas the opposite trait appears infrequently, if at all.

69

CATEGORIES
(Circle all those that apply, skip those that do not apply.)

SLANT

towards right   towards left   vertical slant

extreme right   extreme left   varying or erratic

SIZE OF SCRIPT

small   large   medium   variable

SPACING – Between Words

normal   very narrow   very wide

SPACING – Between Lines

normal   far apart   close to each other

lines tangled

SPACING – Between Letters

normal   very crowded   broad   narrow and crowded

ZONES

inflated upper   compressed upper

inflated lower   compressed lower

inflated middle   compressed middle

PRESSURE

heavy   light   medium

varying heavy and light

GENERAL TYPES

garland   arcade   angular   threaded

(may be a combination of these)

CAPITAL LETTERS

average   small   large

CAPITAL LETTER "I"

inflated   deflated   left-tilting   right-tilting

printed "I" (large straight vertical line)

inflated underloops   flourishes

SMALL LETTER "i"

dot: high above stem   placed before stem   at right of stem
      circled   wavy   dashed   absence of dot
stem: tall and sharp-pointed   loopy   tent-shaped
      arrow-shaped

THE LETTER "t"

For the T-Bar: average balanced crossing   left of stem
     right of stem   above stem   low on stem
     light pressure   heavy pressure
     down-slanted   up-slanted
     short crossing   long crossing   no crossing
     club-like   bowed-bar   inverted bar   "tented"
     return stroke to left   sharp ending   blunt-ending
     knotted   down-turned hook   up-turned hook

For the stem: star-like "t,"   old fashioned "t"

THE LETTERS "a" and "o"
double-looped   open at top   open at bottom
having a lead-in stroke

THE LETTER "b"
bottom portion: open   tightly closed
very loopy top stroke

THE LETTER "c"
"crowns"   loops

THE LETTER "d"
stem: loopy   tall-unlooped   short-unlooped
very tall and wide   split stem   "spoon" stem

THE LETTER "e"
closed loop   broad loop   Greek "E"

THE LETTER "f"
balanced upper and lower parts   no upper loop
large lower loop   angular   fluid form   knotted

THE LETTERS "g," "q," "y" and "z"
stem: long length   overfullness   triangular
loop: none or very narrow long   minimal or incomplete bottom
"g" written like no. "8"   "q" written like no. "9"

THE LOOPS OF LETTERS "h," "k," and "l"
short   narrow/tall   tall and wide   pointed   single line
no loop

THE LETTERS "m" and "n"
rounded   sharp points   initial stroke larger and flourishing
graceful first stroke   final stroke higher than any other

THE LETTER "r"
flat-topped   double-peaked   initial stroke "looped"
parochial "r"

THE LETTER "s"
printed "s"   two or more different types

LOOPS
moderate   exaggerated and loopy   extremely excessive
tall and wide   tall and narrow

EXTRA STROKES
Lead in stroke: long   short   absent
Ending stroke: long   short   absent   ornamental

KNOTS, HOOKS, CLAWS
knotted letters ("t" and "f")   upturned claws and hooks
downturned claws and hooks

MARGINS
wide   narrow   none   uneven *(at right)*   uneven *(at left)*

CONNECTS BETWEEN LETTERS
often   rarely   non-existent

DISCONNECTS BETWEEN LETTERS
often   rarely   non-existent

SIGNATURE

like the script   smaller than script

larger than script   very much larger than script

slants to left (script slants to right)

slants to right (script slants to left or is vertical)

vertical (script vertical or slightly slants to left)   underscoring

illegible (with legible script)   illegible (with illegible script)

encircled   crossed-out   large capitals   small capitals

LINES SLANTS

straight   slant upward   slant downward

TYPE OF SCRIPT (see Chapters 10, 11 and 12)

organized   disorganized   printed   written very quickly

legible   illegible   simple   inconsistent   uniform

wavy   slurry   blotchy or smeary   complex   ornamental

varies in: slant   size   spacing   pressure

Summary and Final Analysis:

Chapter 14
EXAMPLES

EXAMPLE 1

Friendly, charming, likeable, pleasant, gregarious, likes people, likes socializing and entertaining, very sensitive, sympathetic, intuitive.
Active, likes variety/travel, creative, artistic, likes dancing/music.

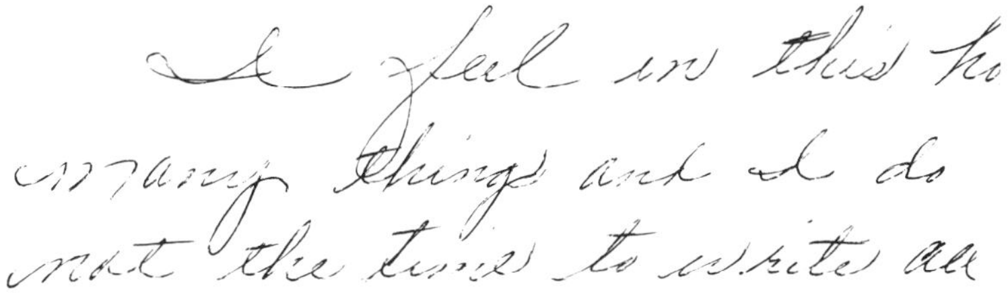

[handwritten text]

EXAMPLE 2

True friend, "beautiful" person, intelligent, good in detail, logical, philosophical, needs "space."
"Pushes" hard, tenacious, go-getter, "plays it big."
Intense personality, emotionally expressive, overinflated ego.
Wonderful when in good mood and hard to get along with when not.
Inflexible in attitude, stubborn, intolerant, impetuous.

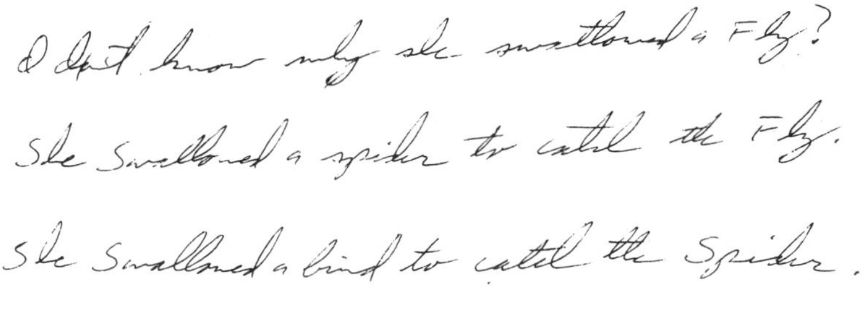

[handwritten text]

EXAMPLE 3

Nice person, gentle, compassionate, gregarious, loves people, sees and makes life lovely, feels for other people and is interested in them individually, looks for good in other people, loves zest of living.

Spontaneous, adventurous, philosophical, very intelligent, great mental comprehension, emotionally expressive, intuitive.

Needs "space," sensitive to criticism, gullible.

I feel free as a bird when I wake in the morning.

EXAMPLE 4

Creative, imaginative, talented, versatile, well-educated, literary, romantic, charming.

Has simple life desires, independent.

Reserved, discriminating, cautious, withdrawn, lacks confidence, a loner, squelched ego, has lost personal self-identity, feels like a loser (probably has had a disasterous past personal relationship(s)).

For the last several yea lived in Newport Beach I had the opportunity down to Laguna, and

76

EXAMPLE 5

Sociable, outgoing, knows cultural amenities, intelligent, controlled, good imagination (although not used to fullest).

Inhibited, repressed, self-centered, confined, unhappy, wants isolation from people, has no life philosophy.

EXAMPLE 6

Friendly, outgoing, generous, "people" oriented, enthusiastic, philosophical, spiritual, intuitive, creative, doesn't like to be idle.

Proud, independent, go-getter, very careful, has physical frailties, irritable when not satisfied, perfectionist, personal pride and need for self-identity, hard to please.

Notes

Chapter 15

THE JOB INTERVIEW: Hiring And Choosing Careers By The Numbers

A. *The Employee*

This chapter will show you that your handwriting should reveal the best job you are suited for and one that you would truly enjoy. Although there are many ways and many books telling you how to determine what job is for you, handwriting analysis is probably the best and fastest one that gives you character evaluation. Graphology reveals your specific talents and aptitudes, such as whether you qualify in management, sales, purchasing, education, law, medicine, the arts, just to mention a few. Are you scientific, have musical or mathematical ability, a flair for dramatics or is your forte in construction, agriculture or working in a factory?

The job for you should be one that complements your interest and faculty for learning as well as for the financial rewards. It is one that should be challenging, one you know or will know and one that you are happy in rather feeling only so-so about, resulting in a feeling of drudgery.

Many of us have a job that we are unhappy with, but live with anyway because the financial rewards are the best we can find. However, handwriting analysis can reveal "hidden" talents which may be unknown to you and which can be very lucrative and self-satisfying.

B. *The Interview*

It goes without saying that at the interview most of us will be dressed and appear at our best. We also will be on our best behavior and many of us will be psychologically sophisticated enough to know what the interviewer is looking for or what he wants to hear. If we are smart and lucky enough we might even have his dossier.

You will be asked a wide range of questions. The impressions of the interviewer are primarily made through appearance, actions and words, usually the very first that are spoken. Sometimes his intuitivenss enters into the picture when he has faith and relies on it. It's scary, but one can fool the interviewer no matter how intelligent or experienced he is. For example, a dishonest, insecure person who is a "social" misfit or even a thief can alter his personality to appear just the opposite, but the good news is that *his handwriting will expose him*.

C. The Interviewer

More often than not, hiring someone can be analogous to throwing darts or gazing into a crystal ball. The interviewer usually makes his decision within the first few minutes of the interview and, furthermore, his judgement is primarily based on how close his thinking is to the one being interviewed, rather than on his qualifications or the needs of the company.

Hiring someone is both complex and an awesome responsibility, not only because of the time and money lost if the wrong person is hired, but because of the adverse "emotional" factors in firing, hiring and replacing for both the interviewer and the employee.

The two methods of job selection are testing and the interview. Polygraph testing is not legally permitted to be used and written and psychological testing are too time-consuming and the results are not known until perhaps it is too late and the damage is done. Obviously, handwriting analysis because it is "done on the spot" and is accurate, is thus the best way.

There are four important factors to consider when making the final hiring decision of the one being interviewed:

1) He must have the qualifications for the job.

2) Is he best suited for the job he is applying for or would he be better off in some other job or field?

3) He must have specific behavioral characteristics which would make him happy in the job. For example, would he be happier working in a small crowded office or in outside sales?

4) How well does he get along with the other employees, that is, does he socially "fit in"?

The first factor is a must – that goes without saying. The other three are revealed using handwriting analysis. It is a fact that those companies, such as in the insurance field, where the "right" people are hired using handwriting analysis, have sales substantially higher than those that do not. It is also a fact that many large companies in most of the Western Countries (excluding the U.S.A.) will not hire anyone without performing this analysis. There's hope yet! Many U.S.A. companies are now starting to do this.

D. *The Application*

Most applications ask for the same information, experience, education, references. For the interviewer, these should be checked out thoroughly for their validity. Also, check the credit background using TRW or other methods. For higher echelon jobs, your attorney or an investigator can probably help you check for any hidden skeletons providing, of course, the records checked are accurate and he has not changed his name.

Most applications will tell you to print the information needed. Although some valuable information can be obtained from this by the experienced graphologist, the other method should be used, that is, through the handwriting sample. Have the applicant write several sentences on the back of the application (or use a separate sheet of unlined paper) on any subject he so desires and, of course, he must sign his name.

Although hs signature appears on the front side of the application, it is best that it is repeated for convenience of analysis. By what is written, you can also check his ingenuity and creativeness at the same time. Now you are ready to analyze. Although initially, you can make a brief analysis, it is best to tell the applicant that you will call him back after you have had a chance to study and analyze it more thoroughly. Yet, there is nothing wrong with hiring someone on the spot if he has the right handwriting for the job.

E. The Three Main Traits To Look For

You want to hire one whose personality and traits most closely match those specified by the job. Obviously, the traits for an assembly-line worker and an executive would be very different. However, there are certain traits which are common denominators for all legitimate jobs. These include honesty, intelligence and the social aspect, that is getting along with others on the job.

1. Honesty

Such writers are categorized as legitimate, sincere, law-abiding, truthful, fair, upright, dedicated, faithful, trustworthy, loyal, courageous, have integrity, are straightforward and are free from fraud, deception, and subterfuge. The script is clear, consistent, simple and legible, has uniform style, a constant firm pressure, even baseline, absence of ornamental writing with extra strokes and has a consistent slant, size, spacing and pressure. In addition, the letters are well formed, the i-dot and t-bar are firm and exact, and there is no over- or under-inflated Capital I. Also, the three zones are evenly balanced.

Loops — are not ink-filled, double- or triple- over-inflated, excessively backward, lopsided, tangled, complicated or blotchy.

Strokes — there are no prolonged, left-tendency finals, unusual lead-in (especially those that start from below baseline). (Refer to Chapter 9 on how to tell if one is dishonest.)

2. Intelligence

In writing, no simple curlicue or squiggle can capture one's true intelligence. An intelligent person is one who has most, if not all, of the following traits and can communicate his thoughts simply and directly; is organized, objective, intuitive, logical, pragmatic, mentally flexible, has a good memory and reasoning power, and can concentrate. (Refer to Chapter 10 on how to determine this.) The more of these traits one has, the more intelligent.

3. Getting Along With Others On The Job

No one will argue that getting along with your co-workers, including your employer is of the utmost importance, especially since most companies have their own internal politics and undoubtedly a wide range of individual personalities. There are hundreds of psychology books on this subject and no attempt will be made to delve deeply into it here. However, as a guide it can be broken down into five categories.

(1) Thoughtfullness – helping others get what they want. Be altruistic.

(2) Cheerful, pleasant, merry and gratifying – being nice to others, feeling secure within yourself and that others are not trying to harm you.

(3) Understanding – being the peacemaker, by seeing the others point of view and being sympathetic to it. Have the intelligence and awareness to step in at the right time.

(4) Cooperation – go along with the system by not fighting it even though you may disagree with it.

(5) Communication – transmit, accept and exchange messages whether they are verbal, written or gestures.

For the aforementioned, the handwriting should contain the following: (Although it is highly unlikely that it will have all of the following, it should have a great deal of these. The more the better.)

The script should be right-slanting, clear, consistent, simple, neat and legible (a combination of both cursive and script printing is very desirable). Garland and arcade types are the best. The margins should be evenly spaced making it appear like a framed picture. The writing should be of medium size having even spacing between words, letters and lines as well as having equal "zones."

Pressure should be medium and consistent. Capitals should be large. The capital letter "I" should be as simplistic as possible (one tall single line is the best). The letter "t" should have a firm average balanced crossing about the center of the bar. The letters "a" and "o" (and the tops of "p," "q," and "g") should be very slightly open. All loops should be moderate, having no extra strokes with the absence of knots, hooks, and claws. The signature should be easily read and resemble very closely the script.

In most professions, leadership is extremely desirable especially in the executive and managerial areas. Leadership traits are categorized and explained in Chapter 11 and include determination, confidence, communication, sense of humor and self-starting.

F. The Job That Fits You And Which You Would Enjoy The Most

Although your handwriting may reveal the type of job you would best excel in, you may find yourself in a completely different one, even being very successful in it. However, in this case, ask yourself "Am I happy in it?" The chances are that the answer is "no." Therefore, start thinking of a possible change, since the happier you are in a job the better you can perform with the financial rewards coming naturally.

Extreme caution must be exercised in that the following

associated categories are not necessarily and absolutely fully complete since there are many other facets of a script too numerous and complex to be listed here. Using a limited number of categories only tells part of the story. For a complete and thorough analysis, it is suggested that you use an experienced graphologist.

Because of the individual complexity of all of us, it would be foolhardy to say, for example, that all accountants write small. Undoubtedly, there are some accountants that write large. This, of course, does not change their ability in being a good accountant. However, if an accountant does write small, the chances are he excels in working with details. To contain all of the traits listed in a particular category would be ideal. In any case, the more the better.

For a particular job, only those categories which are most likely to prevail are listed. In other words, the odds are that for a particular job the listed category is properly matched to the type of job. If a category is not listed for a particular job it simply means that it is not likely to be dominant in the handwriting, although it may be seen occasionally in the script.

G. Careers By The Numbers – Categories

1. Right Slant

Extroverted, warm personality, communicative, affectionate, amicable, compassionate, gregarious, courageous, expressive, sensitive, sympathetic, future- and goal-oriented, lives life with "zest," always wants "something going on," self-reliant, secure, self-controlled, easily vents feelings.

2. Vertical (Or Slightly To Right) Slant

Ambivert, restrained, emotions in check, independent, self-reliant, secure, self-controlled.

3. Small Size

Meticulous, great in "detail" work, restrained, reticent, perfectionist, resourceful, thrifty, reluctant, mentally academic, doesn't seek limelight, good organizer, good executive ability.

4. Large Size

Bold, aggressive, thinks "big," confident, strongly motivated and directs others, approaches life in an extroverted and exaggerated manner, enthusiastic, optimistic.

5. Slow Writing

Slow but logical thinker, conventional, cautious, precise, careful, hidden feelings, over-controlled.

6. Fast Writing

Fast thinker, very intelligent, intellectual, alert, perceptive.

7. Spacing Between Words And Lines Same Width As Middle Zone Letters

Represents physical and mental contact (or distance) between one's self and others (society). The more equal they are, the better.

8. Lines Separated And Evenly Spaced

Personal harmony, flexible, proper balancing, orderliness, clarity of thought.

9. Very Narrow Spacing between Letters And Words

Needs contact and closeness with others, introverted, can work in "close quarters," good concentration, cautious.

10. Very Wide Spacing between Letters And Words

Need for "inner" privacy and space, has a tendency for isolation, wants to maintain "social" distance, outgoing, uninhibited.

11. Tall Upper Zone

Great imagination, intellectual, spiritual, philosophical, thinks in abstract.

12. Compressed Upper Zone

Little interest in mental, spiritual or philosophical thought, lacks imagination and creativity, nonintellectual.

13. Light Pressure

Fragile and delicate feelings, sensitive personality, more tolerant.

14. Medium To Heavy Pressure

High energy and intensity of thought, aggressive, possessive, go-getter, success-oriented.

15. Angular Writing

Substitutes intellect for emotions, analytical, firm, logical, steadfast, goal-oriented, energetic, shrewd, determined to succeed, competitive.

16. Graceful And Rounded Writing

Charming, gentle, non-aggressive, obedient, even-tempered, gracious, flexible, diplomatic, socially adaptable, pleasure-loving, likeable, kind, outgoing, sympathetic.

15. Angular Writing

Substitutes intellect for emotions, analytical, firm, logical, steadfast, goal-oriented, energetic, shrewd, determined to succeed, competitive.

17. Large Capitals

High confidence, vanity, constructive (when printed).

18. Large Capital "I"

Great ego, very secure, inflated feeling of self-image and self-worth.

19. "a" and "o" (and top portions of "p," "g," and "q") Slightly Open At Top

Open, outgoing, talkative, gullible, generous.

20. "a" and "o" (and top portions of "p," "g," and "q") Tightly Closed

Secretive, cautious, sly.

21. Some Letters Look Like Numbers (e.g., "g" looks like "8" or "9"; "o's" are perfect circles)

Mathematically inclined, works with and is good in arithmetic and math.

22. Strong And Long "T" Bars Centered Above Half-Way On Stem

Ambitious, determined, self-controlled, has will-power, firm

23. Wide And Long Lower Loops

Extreme desire to satisfy physical and sexual desires, great interest in food and money.

24. Narrow And Long Lower Loops

Wants to satisfy physical and sexual desires, very practical.

25. No Loops In Lower Extensions

Practical, simple tastes, determined, firm, aggressive.

26. Wide Left Margin And Narrow Right Margin

Avoids the past and has courage facing future.

27. Narrow Left Margin And Wide Right Margin

Avoids the future, is reserved.

H. Analysis Of Jobs And Professions By Categories
(Numbers shown are referencing the categories listed on the previous pages.)

Accountant   2,3,9,21
Actor   1,4,8,14,16,17,18,19
Advertising   1,4,11,14,17,18,19

Agriculture Work   7,26
Artist (simple, rythmic script)   8,11,14,16
Assembly-Line Work   12,27
Attorney   1,4,6,8,15,17,20,25
Author – (nonfiction)   1,6,11,14,17,18
Author – (fiction)   3,6,14,15,17,18,21
Bank Teller   2,6,9,21
Bartender   1,4,7,12,16,19,24,26
Bookkeeper   2,3,9,20,21
Budget Director   2,3,9,20,21
Cashier   2,3,20,21
Caterer   1,6,8,17,19,23
Checker (supermarket)   2,3,20,21
Clergy   1,4,6,7,8,11,16,17,18,19
Clerical Work   3,8,21
Computer Programmer   2,3,14,17,20,21,27
Construction Work   4,12,23,27
Contractor   3,6,7,8,14,17,18,22
Conservation Work   4,7,8,17,18,19,26
Cook   5,23
Court Reporter   2,3,6,7,8,13,16,20,27
Craftsman   4,7,8,17,18,19,26
Dentist   2,3,6,11,14,15,17,18,20,22,25
Designer   3,8,17,18,20
Desk Clerk   1,4,7,8,16,19,25
Detective   4,6,7,8,11,14,17,18,20,22
Diplomat   1,4,6,8,14,16,17,18,20,26
Doctor   2,3,6,11,14,15,17,18,20,22,25
Dramatics (writing has simple "open" appearance)
   1,4,11,17,18,19,26
Editor   2,3,6,7,9,14,15,22
Engineer   2,3,6,9,14,17,20,21

Entertainer 1,4,6,7,14,16,17,19,26
Executive 2,3,6,8,11,14,17,18,20,21,22,25,26
Food Critic 1,8,11,14,15,17,18,19,22,23
Forest Ranger 1,4,14,16,26
Heavy Equipment Operator 2,12,24,27
Hermit 2,10,12,13,20,27
Historian 2,3,6,12,14,20,27
Hostess 2,3,6,12,14,20,27
Housewife 1,4,7,13,16,19,23
Interior Decorator 1,4,8,11,17,18,26
Inventor 2,3,7,9,11,14,15,20,22,26
Journalist 1,6,8,14,17,18,26
Librarian 2,3,7,9,13,15,20,27
Loan Officer 2,6,9,15,20,21,26
Lumberjack 12,24,27
Manager 2,3,6,14,15,17,18,20
Manual Labor 5,12,27
Marathon Runner 12,17,22,24
Mathematician 2,3,6,9,14,17,20,21
Mechanic 2,12,20,24
Musician (simple rythmic script) 8,11,14,16
Nurse 1,7,8,14,16,19
Philosopher 1,4,7,11,13,16,17
Pilot 2,3,6,10,14,17,22,24
Poet 1,4,7,8,11,14,17,27
Policeman 1,2,4,6,14,15,17,19
Politician 1,4,6,8,14,15,16,17,18,20,26
Professor 3,6,7,11,14,15
Psychologist 6,7,8,11,14,17,18
Public Servant 1,4,7,8,13
Public Relations 1,4,6,7,8,11,14,17,18,26
Physicist 2,3,6,9,14,17,20,21

Researcher   2,3,6,7,8,11,14,15,20
Real Estate Agent   1,4,7,8,14,16,17,19,26
Receptionist   1,4,7,8,13,16,19,26
Sales   1,4,6,10,14,16,17,18,19,26
Sales Engineer (combination of sales and engineer)
Scientist (see Researcher)
Secretary   1,2,3,6,7,8,13,16
Sexual Surrogate   12,16,17,18,19,22,24
Sports Player   12,17,22,24
Statistican   2,3,6,9,14,15,17,18,20,21,22
Student   2,5,8,12,27
Supervisor (see Manager)
Teacher   1,3,6,7,15,17
Technician (see Engineer)
Tool Maker   2,3,5,12,20,21,27
Travel Agent   1,2,7,8,16,19,22
Treasurer   2,3,6,9,14,17,18,20
Waiter   1,4,7,12,16,19,24,26
Warehouse Worker   2,5,14,21,24,27
Watchmaker   2,5,12,20
Worker (outdoors)   4,12,14,19,23
Writer (see Author)

Example of "Author (nonfiction)"

The following script was written by a famous author-publisher (Para-Publishing) of over 20 best-selling nonfiction books. Checking categories 3,6,14,15,17,18,21, we can see his writing is relatively small, quick, heavy-pressured and angular. His capitals are large, including "I." Also, some of the letters look like numbers (note in the word "interesting" the g looks like a 9).

Thus, we can evaluate him as being meticulous, a perfectionist, resourceful, thrifty, a fast thinker, very intelligent as well as shrewd, intellectual, alert, perceptive, has high energy and intensity of thought, aggressive, go-getter, success-oriented, energetic, determined to succeed, competitive, is very confident, constructive, has a great ego, and is very secure.

Jess —

Many thanks for coming to our workshop this past weekend. It was a great group & you have a very interesting book.

Here are a few sentences + yes you have

Dan _____

Chapter 16

HOW TO CHOOSE THE RIGHT MATE, LOVER OR FRIEND

Handwriting analysis is not a substitute for counseling or psychologic or psychiatric guidance when it comes to choosing the right mate, lover or friend. Rather it is simply a quick way of getting a thumbnail sketch as to compatibility and disclosing the behavior and personality of another. It is interesting to note that some computer dating services are using handwriting analysis as an additonal aid in helping to choose a partner.

The analysis should be used *before* dating or developing a relationship. In that way there are no surprises as to what the future will bring. Think of the time and energy you have spent in the past developing relationships, only to find out that your partner wasn't for you. Even if you rely on your intuitiveness, or have one checked out, you can't be absolutely sure of his personality and behavior until it might be too late, unless you use handwriting analysis.

What are you looking for in the opposite sex?

Here are some important traits we probably would all like in a partner: ambition, intelligence, good lover, very secure, stable, generous, humorous, gentle, protective, responsible, communicative, likeable, compassionate, and honest. There are others that may be especially important only to you. All of these can be found in the handwriting analysis.

Ask yourself these questions: Even if you do discover

the traits you seek in writing, are they compatible with yours, or what if you possess many adverse ones? Which of the undesirable traits would you tolerate? Do you always pick the same kind of person to be involved with? Is he looking for a father or mother image? Is he selfish or is there a give and take? Will the relationship turn out to be primarily sex-oriented or is there more? Who has the better money sense and can handle the budget? Who should be the leader during emotional storms? What common interests are there? The answers to these and countless others are answered by the analysis.

Simply, compatibility is accomplished by comparing the two handwritings. Analyze the two separate writings individually and then start comparing them. Several examples are given here showing how this is done using various handwriting types.

When the writings are similar in an overall way it is obvious that the two are compatible. When they are very similar, the relationship becomes sound but may end up to be boring. This does not necessarily imply that when they are dissimilar they are not compatible; in fact such a relationship can be quite interesting. It depends upon how dissimilar they are, the particular facet, how important the facets are to each, and how much effort one is willing to give to try to change it.

Emotionally we are all in a constant state of flux. To prove this point, save your handwriting over the years, keeping a diary and dates, and watch how it changes. As you change, and most of us do, so does your handwriting. This would show how, when and if one person *outgrows* another.

You should periodically compare your writing with your mate to see in which areas the handwriting has changed and then try to compensate and change it. Without this analysis, the changes may be very subtle and barely noticeable, especially after living with one over a long period of time. This procedure could very well prevent a possible split up.

It would be too volumnous to give every possible combination of handwriting types to compare and analyze. Four examples are given to *guide* you through how this is done.

Example 1

Referring to Figure 1, she is: gentle, easy-going, conserves energy as much as possible, emotions under control, likes to be physical, gentle, intuitive, very quick-thinking mind and altruistic. A very nice person indeed!

He (Figure 2) has a tremendous amount of energy for himself and others. A human dynamo! Very emotional about himself and others. He is not self-sensitive, has lots of confidence, a sharp mind, a good ego, very secure, well-organized, extroverted, is more logical than intuitive, honest.

Both are very compatible and get along very well with each other since one complements the other. He is the ambitious go-getter, emotional-intense type, involving himself with others, getting things done in a very clear manner, whereas she has the *calming* effect on the relationship, being gentle and understanding in emotional situations. The fact is in real life they are very happily married.

Figure 1

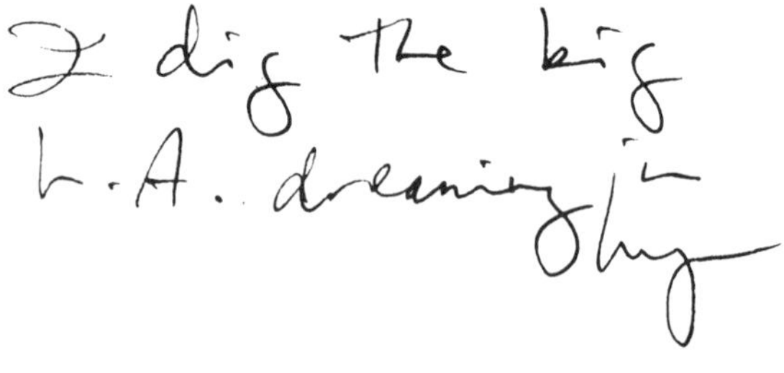

Figure 2

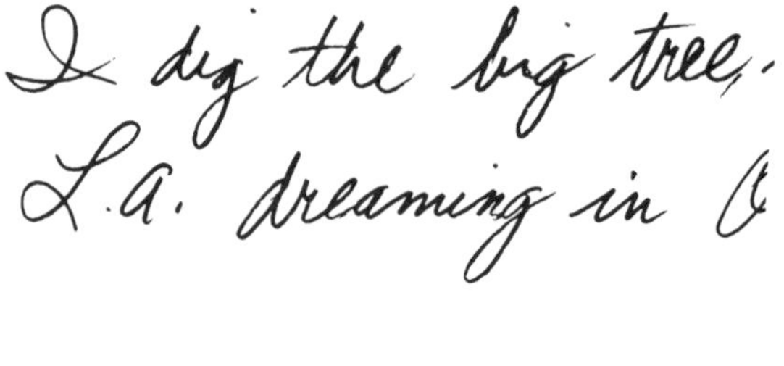

Example 2

Note how similar the writings are in Figure 3 (she) and Figure 4 (he). Both are slanted to the right, write large with medium pressure, both thrive on begin physical and mental. They are easy going and gentle and for the most part won't create problems in a relationship. This means they see eye-to-eye on most issues. They have the common interest in meeting and being with other people and could easily develop new relationships with a minimum of effort. Each would be happy to do their own thing, yet enjoy the moments they are with each other. Since they are both generous, cordial and out-going, very little friction would develop between them in a relationship and would probably be happy in a marriage, although care would have to be taken not to be bored with each other.

Figure 3

This is a lovely Sunday & I'm happy

Figure 4

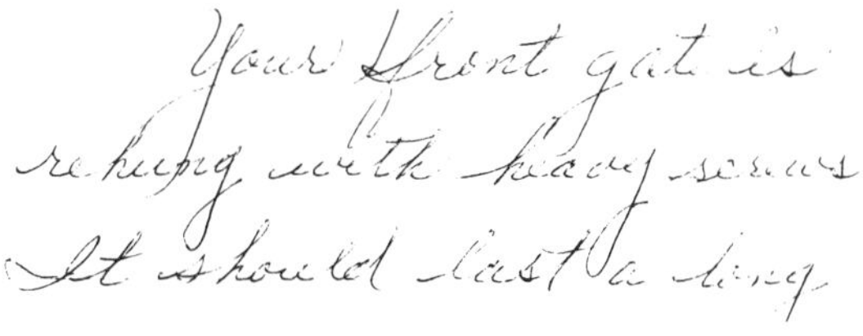

Your front gate is reHeading with heavy serves. It should last a long

Example 3

In Figure 5 (she) slants her writing to the left indiciating she has a tendency to be introverted, reserved, and well-controlled. However, she is also very gentle, gracious and is a very sensitive person who requires lots of attention and worries a lot.

On the other hand, he (Figure 6) has a very strong and emotional personality, having a tendency to be argumentative, high pressured, unsympathetic, abrupt and can be sarcastic. She could probably survive sufficiently enough being with others. He, on the other hand, would like to be with others, but might have difficulty maintaining meaningful relationships. It is obvious that these two are very much the opposites and would have a very difficult time in maintaining a happy marriage. The obstacles to overcome would be extremely difficult.

Figure 5

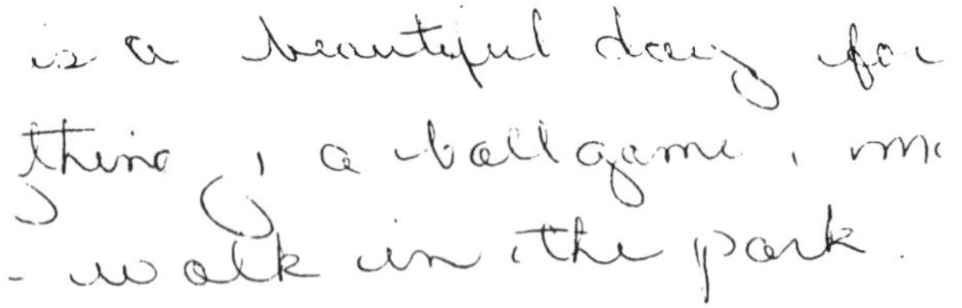

Figure 6

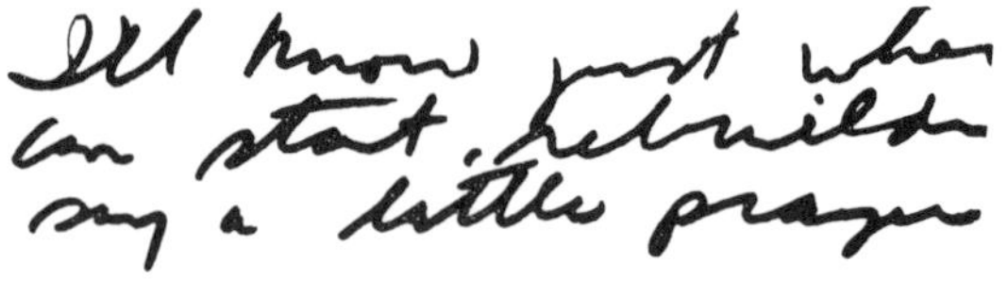

Example 4

In this example, she (Figure 7) is extroverted, has a warm personality, can communicate, is affectionate, amicable, sensitive, sympathetic and loves to be with people. He (Figure 8), on the other hand, with his small vertical writing indicates that he is restrained, secure, modest, reticent, a perfectionist, resourceful and thrifty.

Obviously, both are completely different from each other. Whereas she wants and needs people and needs conversation and attention, he would sooner put himself in isolation. Getting along with each other on a consistent basis would be extremely difficult. Marriage is important to her but not to him. There is very little chance that such a relationship would ultimately succeed.

Figure 7

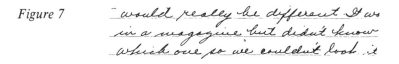

Figure 8

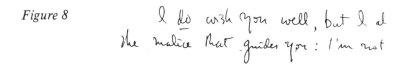

Notes

Chapter 17

HEALTH, DRUGS AND ALCOHOL
(Graphotherapeutics)

There has been much written about the relationship between handwriting and health, including the use of drugs and alcohol. This subject is called *graphotherapeutics*. Because of its complexity and because much research is still going on and since much must be learned about it, it will only be discussed briefly here, covering some of the highlights.

Graphotherapeutics is exremely important. Can you imagine how great a revelation it is for you or someone you know to discover a previously unknown ailment? This is also extremely valuable in the hiring of employees, knowing, for example, if they are habitual users of drugs or alcohol, making them unfit for proper continuous functional performance. This in no way implies that handwriting analysis diagnoses diseases. It simply *warns* you that a health problem may prevail and should be looked into. It also warns you about drug and alcohol users.

How it works is very simple. Your brain sends signals throughout your body when there is either a physical or mental health problem. This then is reflected through your nervous system and into your hands and fingers and, of course, your handwriting. It is interesting to note that records show that in many cases one's handwriting changes radically immediately before death, in a way depending upon the cause of it.

For what it's worth, in most cases the writing indications of ailments including drug and alcohol users are very similar to one's handwriting that shows dishonesty (Chapter 9).

Care must be taken not to confuse the two.

If there is a question of hiring someone who can be either in bad health, a user or drugs or alcohol, or dishonest, the best thing to do is, of course, not hire that person to be safe. Conversely, it stands to reason that one in good health and not a drug or alcohol user writes like an honest person. That is, the script is smooth, rhythmic, the strokes are continuous and well formed, there is even pressure and the baseline is firm and straight. The exception to the aforementioned is one who has a permanent nerve, muscle or brain injury which would offset the controlling of normal hand movement. Don't confuse such a person with a dishonest one.

You could alert yourself to the danger of developing an illness by watching any unexplained and suspicious changes of your own handwriting. This is why handwriting records that are dated should be kept periodically. For example, if over the years you normally write in a clear even-handed way and find that your writing gradually or even suddenly becomes unclear, diffused, haphazard, and disorganized you could be a candidate for a mental breakdown.

It is interesting to note that some sick people make their t-bars longer and stronger as their will to live becomes stronger. Omitting details like i-dots or punctuation and could be noticed through fear of death and because of anxiety.

A. *The Drug Addict*

Drug addicts (and alcoholics) want to escape from the real world and into one that is not. Because the drug addict has lost control so-to-speak, his handwriting reflects just this. For those who are not particularly heavy drug users look for the following symptoms:

1. The writing is not rythmic.
2. The baseline is wavy or uneven.
3. Mistakes are made in spelling and punctuation.
4. Bottom loops are wider than normal and there are larger connecting strokes.

For those who are major drug users, the disintegration of the writing becomes more obvious.
1. Confused writing where words and letters run into each other.
2. Descending baseline.
3. Jerky writing with extreme right-hand slant.
4. Varied pressure (writing looks blotchy), slant and rhythm of writing.
5. Weirdly-shaped letters.
6. Double or even triple-looped letters such as for the y, g, or p.
7. Intermixed angular and round-shaped letters.
8. Some letters are much smaller than others.
9. "Swirls" at the beginning of capital letters (looks like a spring) indicating secrecy.
10. Sometimes letters in words are only partially written, re-written, retraced several times or are tangled.
11. Weird mistakes in spelling.
12. Light or absence of T-bars.

B. *The Alcoholic*

The following will show that the alcoholic's writing is very similar in many respects to that of the drug addict. The alcoholic, like the drug user, wants to shut out the real world and to escape reality. Alcoholics have a poor self-image, are critical and emotionally erratic. It is important to note that all alcoholics do not necessarily show the following signs in their handwriting, but at least it will show several of these. Look for the following in their writing:

1. Lack of rhythm since their muscular coordination is poor.
2. Inability to write on an even slant due to mental deterioration.
3. Extreme right-slanted or left-slanted writing.
4. Writing may be legible but it is written very quickly and is muddy.
5. Baseline descends and it varies, showing depression.
6. The rhythm and quality of the writing is jerky and lacks quality, indicating being "disturbed."
7. Writing is sloppy containing many mistakes.
8. There are variations in pressure showing instability.
9. Unnatural breaks in the words.
10. Sloppy writing with many misspelled words.
11. "Hooks" and "daggers" in the T-bar and in the baseline.
12. Weak, short and varied T-bars.
13. Short capitals, especially the letter "I."

C. *Emotional and Mental Disturbances*

Because handwriting is the hypersensitive link to the brain, emotional and mental disturbances are readily seen in the script. One might say handwriting is "brain" writing. If the mind is void of reality, the handwriting will not be able to be read at all. Consider the case when the mind is conscious of the environment but is confused and restless. In its simplest form such an emotionally disturbed person going through a chaotic life change writes in a confused way, that is, lines and words in the script run into one another. A prelude to a mental disorder might be melancholia. Such a person might write with a descending baseline and the pointing down or drooping of the last word of the line.

Some indications of possible emotional and mental disorders include:

1. The writing is illegible, slanted in all directions and has inconsistent baselines runing into each other, showing confusion.
2. The rhythm of the script is exaggerated and has excessive punctuation, for example, double i-dots and double-crossed T's.
3. Writing descends.
4. Extreme left- or right-slant.
5. Pressure tends to be either very heavy, very light or varied.
6. Varying word and letter sizes and small letters used in place of large ones.
7. Spacing of words is inconsistent and is out of proportion.
8. Tendency for involved flourishes, repeated and underlined words.
9. A variety of different types of T-bars including those that are awkward, illegible, diffused and those that do not go through the stem – indicating guilt feelings.
10. Exaggerated and entangled upper and lower loops.

D. *Physical Illness*

There is absolutely no intention here of using hand-writing analysis as a diagnostic tool. Rather it should be used to make one aware that an illness could possibly exist and one should seek medical advice. The following lists some of the types of ailments.

Heart Disease — The symptoms include interruptions or breaks in the up and down strokes, especially in the loops of letters. Abnormal dotting of stem letters 'i" and "j" indicates that the writer wants to rest and catch his breath. Also, partial dotting of these letters is indicative of the inability to correlate one's movements.

Problems of the Brain — In such cases, the writing is different in each and every case, depending upon the specific problem. For example, consider the paranoid who is suspicious that people are plotting against him and is disoriented as to time and place. His handwriting might be highlighted, to have very wide spacing between words, capital letters are placed where they don't belong, the "i's" and "j's" are extremely broad, and the finals are exaggerated, indicating the exaggeration of his thoughts.

Middle Body Injury — You probably guessed this one! The writing, including the size and shape of the letters, is erratic, broken and repaired or attempted to be repaired, in the middle zone. Also some of the words are depressed.

Cancer — Since cancer can strike in any part of the body, it is in the occurring zone which will show some type of distortion in the handwriting. One must be extremely cautious to come to any definite conclusions when suspecting cancer. This is one area that much research in handwriting remains to be done. There are some texts which do go into great detail on this subject giving specific case histories. In any case, one symptom seems to crop up, that is, that some parts of the writing appear to have "hairy" line distortions as if the pen has picked up a piece of lint.

Partial Eyesight — Cataracts fall into this category. Usually the script is not clearly written which is obvious enough. Many letters are retraced since the writer doesn't see them clearly showing complusiveness. You might find some of the T-bars bowed like an umbrella and perhaps hooked on the end.

Nerve Damage — The writing has inconsistent pressure with jerky strokes. The spacing between words is erratic and the letter forms are slow and over-controlled.

Polio — Consider the victim who cannot straighten his legs out and walk and, therefore, limps. The jerky rhythm of his writing represents stiffness with which the lower limbs are used. The upper loops are compressed indicating his attention to the lower area of his body and to escape the reality of pain.

The following are some examples of physical ailments.

Distorted letter formations could indicate a possible back problem.

Loops that are broken near the top and/or ragged on the side could indicate a heart problem.

Loops that are broken at the very top could signal mental problems or something in the upper part of the body.

Loops that are broken in the lower zone could signal problems in the lower part of the body, such as a hernia or menstruating difficulty.

This could very well be the writing of a "stroke" victim.

Chapter 18
CHANGE YOUR HANDWRITING–
CHANGE YOURSELF
(Graphotherapy)

In handwriting, your nervous system acts as a wire from brain to hand where the hand acts only as the vehicle doing what the brain tells it to do. If the reverse process occurs, the hand then dictates to the brain. Thus, by changing your handwriting (which is physical) you change your mind (which is mental). This process is called graphotherapy. At first thought, it would appear that this would be highly unlikely to occur. Why not? We do it all the time. For example, if we were to lift extra heavy weights (physical), which we normally don't do, we send a message to our brain to prevail (mental). Our brain then responds to our physical desire.

Psychiatry and psychology accomplish the changing of a trait through complex techniques and exercises in conjunction with expensive equipment. *Graphotherapy does the same thing simply and quickly just using a pen or a pencil by not only identifying the problem, but helping solve it.* Graphotherapy is not an untested theory, it is a proven psychological aid.

To change a trait takes a great persistence and repetition and is accomplished only after your brain yields to the power of your hand. Although several traits can be changed simultaneously, it is best to change only one trait at a time since it is less confusing. You should be able to notice the emergence of the desirable trait you are trying to acquire and eliminate the one you want to dispose of in about 30 days, although it may take as much as six months to master it finally and completely.

How to Make The Change

We look for a reason to make a change. One way of doing this is by seeking goals, letting ourselves know what we want to accomplish. In this way we will be constantly reminded of it.

Changing a trait requires that you write a pre-determined sentence(s) at least 5 or 10 times a day (the more the better) depicting the actual change you are making. You must constantly give it your full and utmost attention, clearly focusing on this with no interruptions unless you drift away from the purpose and resort to the old way of writing. This is one reason why it takes so long to accomplish this and why you must be persistent. The chances are that it has taken years, maybe even a lifetime to develop an adverse trait so you can't expect to eliminate it overnight.

At the beginning it will be difficult to manage since it is a new physical adjustment, like learning a new exercise. However, by making it habitual, you will develop perfection. Of course, your subconscious mind will soon enter the picture making both the physical and mental work simultaneously. This is analogous to playing a guitar, for example, where you play it both physically and mentally, unlike when you first learned to play it when it was mostly mechanical. In time it becomes automatic.

Design the sentence in a positive vein that depicts the trait you want to develop. The following lists seven examples of traits many of us would like to obtain by eliminating those we want to dispose of.

1. **Present script:** Relatively short capitals, especially the capital letter "I," light pressure.

Characteristics: Insecurity, lack of self-esteem and confidence.

Solution: Make all of the capitals much higher, writing with heavier pressure.

Sentence to write; "I will write using heavier pressure and increase the size of the capitals and my pronoun "I" to give me a better picture of my security, self-esteem and confidence."
Sign your name (Indicate the date each time yo do this for a date diary.)

2. **Present script: Left-slanted writing.**

   Characteristics: Writer tends to be cautious, suspicious, introverted, withdrawn, unfriendly, etc.

   Solution: Write right-slanted.

   Sentence to write; "It will be easier for me to communicate with other people and be more extroverted if I write with a right-slant."

   Sign your name (and date)

3. **Present script: Letters "d" and "t" short and wide looped (The loops are wider than that of the closest letter "e.")**

   Characteristics: Writer is over self-sensitive

   Solution: Write "d's" and "t's" taller and without loops

   Sentence to write; "I understand that the letters "d" and "t" must be written tall and without loops to reduce my self-sensitivity."

   Sign your name (and date)

4. **Present script: The bar of the letter "t" starts crossing at or near the stem and extends to the right of it.** *(It might also be found that the dots of "i's" and "j's"appear at the far right of the stem.)*

   Characteristics: Writer is impulsive, that is, he acts momentarily without due thought.

   Solution: Cross "t's" at the center of stem and dot "i's" and "j's" directly above the stem.

   Sentence to write; *"I will not be impulsive and act momentarily without due thought before making a decision by crossing my "t's" at the center of stem and dotting "i's" and "j's" directly above the stem.*

   Sign your name (and date)

5. **Present script: The bar of the letter "t" starts crossing at or near the stem and extends to the left of it.** (It might be found that the dots of "i's" and "j's" appear at the far left of the stem.)

   Characteristics: Writer procrastinates, that is, he puts off making decisions for fear of failing.

   Solution: Cross "t's" at the center of the stem and dot "i's" and "j's" directly above the stem.

   Sentence to write; *"I will not procrastinate and put off making decisions for fear of failing by crossing my "t's" at the center of the stem and dotting "i's" and "j's" directly above the stem.*

   Sign your name (and date)

6. **Present script: The letters within words are frequently separated from each other.**

114

Characteristics: The writer is intuitive and has an immediate and instinctive perception of a truth. However, he prefers to think in a more logical rather than in an intuitive way.

Solution: All letters within words should be interconnected leaving no interruptions or spaces.

Sentence to write; "I must interconnect all of the letters within the words I write leaving no interruptions or spaces and thus think in a more logical way."

Sign your name (and date)

7. **Present script: The letters within words are interconnected and are not separated.**

Characteristics: The writer is a logical thinker having pure and formal thought. However, he prefers to think in a more intuitive rather than in a more logical way.

Solution: Most letters of words should be broken or interrupted.

Sentence to write; "I must not interconnect all letters of the words I write, leaving as many interruptions as possible, and thus think in a more intuitive way."

Sign your name (and date)

The above format can be used to change your script and develop any characteristic you wish. For example, why not work one up for better sexuality?

Notes

To Order Your Handwriting Analysis. . .

Enclosed are _____ writing samples with
signature(s), to analyzed at $20.00 per sample. $_____

Plus tax or other
(sales tax-CA res. add 6.75%, $_____
Canada- add $2.00, overseas-$3.00)

Total enclosed $_____

Make check or money order payable to:
Pantex International Ltd., P. O. Box 17322, Irvine, CA 92713.

Please print or type:

Name_____

Address_____

City_____ State_____ Zip_____

Age_____ Sex: M or F _____ Right- or Left-handed _____

NOTE: Please copy this form for additional analyses.

To Order Additional Copies of This Book. . .

1 copy $15.95
2 - 4 copies........... $13.95 ea
5 or more .... $11.95 ea
Over 10 copies, contact publisher for pricing.

No. of copies   _____
Price/copy $_____ =   _____
Sales Tax (CA res. 6.75%)   _____
Shipping: *US–$2, Canada–$3, Overseas–$5* _____
Total Enclosed $_____

Allow 4 - 6 weeks for delivery.

To Have Your Handwriting Analyzed. . . .

Complete the following handwriting sample, including your signature. If you use different signatures, include all of them. Use your regular writing and DO NOT PRINT. If necessary, use a sheet of unlined paper.

"I would like to know what my handwriting reveals about my behavior and personality. Mostly I would like to disclose my physical and material drives, emotional strengths and weaknesses. Thank you for the opportunity for helping me understand myself better."   (sign your name)

_____

To Order Your Handwriting Analysis. . .

Enclosed are _____ writing samples with
signature(s), to analyzed at $20.00 per sample. $_____

Plus tax or other
(sales tax-CA res. add 6.75%, $_____
Canada- add $2.00, overseas-$3.00)

Total enclosed $_____

Make check or money order payable to:
Pantex International Ltd., P. O. Box 17322, Irvine, CA 92713.

Please print or type:

Name_____

Address_____

City_____ State_____ Zip_____

Age_____ Sex: M or F _____ Right- or Left-handed _____

NOTE: Please copy this form for additional analyses.

To Order Additional Copies of This Book. . .

1 copy $15.95
2 - 4 copies .... $13.95 ea
5 or more .... $11.95 ea
Over 10 copies, contact publisher for pricing.

No. of copies   _____
Price/copy $_____ =   _____
Sales Tax (CA res. 6.75%)   _____
Shipping: *US–$2, Canada–$3, Overseas–$5*   _____
Total Enclosed $_____

Allow 4 - 6 weeks for delivery.

To Have Your Handwriting Analyzed. . . .

Complete the following handwriting sample, including your signature. If you use different signatures, include all of them. Use your regular writing and DO NOT PRINT. If necessary, use a sheet of unlined paper.

"I would like to know what my handwriting reveals about my behavior and personality. Mostly I would like to disclose my physical and material drives, emotional strengths and weaknesses. Thank you for the opportunity for helping me understand myself better."

(sign your name)

main

155.282 D585 c.1
Dines, Jess E.
Handwriting analysis made
easy

PORTLAND PUBLIC LIBRARY
5 MONUMENT SQ.
PORTLAND, ME 0410

WITHDRAWN

DATE DUE		
MAY 20 1998	AUG 0 8 2000	
DEC 15 1998	AUG 07 200	
MAY 01 1999		6
MAY 22 1999	AUG 1 1 2003	
JUL 06 1999	FEB 0 9 2005	8
JUL 20 1999	JUN 1 4 2005	6
OCT 2 8 1999	NOV 1 0 2005	
MAR 3 0 2000		